The
Courageous
Patriot

Idella Bodie

SANDLAPPER PUBLISHING CO., INC.

Second Printing, 2005

Published by Sandlapper Publishing Co., Inc.
 Orangeburg, South Carolina USA

Heroes and Heroines of the American Revolution Series

Manufactured in the United States of America

Library of Congress Cataloging-in-Publication Data

Bodie, Idella.
     The courageous patriot / by Idella Bodie.
        p. cm. — (Heroes and heroines of the American Revolution)
     Includes bibliographical references (p.) and index.
     ISBN 0-87844-157-3

     1. Motte, Rebecca Brewton, 1737-1815—Juvenile literature. 2.
Women revolutionaries—United States—Biography—Juvenile
literature. 3. Revolutionaries—United States—Biography—Juvenile
literature. 4. Charleston (S.C.)—History—Revolution, 1775-1783—
Juvenile literature. 5. Charleston (S.C.)—Biography—Juvenile
literature. 6. United States—History—Revolution, 1775-1783—
Biography—Juvenile literature. [1. Motte, Rebecca Brewton, 1737-
1815. 2. Revolutionaries. 3. United States—History—Revolution,
1775-1783. 4. Women—Biography.] I. Title.

E207 M84 B63 2001
973.3'092—dc21
[B]

                                                    2001020099

IN THE SUMMER OF 1781, Patriot officers General Francis Marion and Colonel Henry Lee tried without success to remove the British from Fort Motte. Their artillery could not penetrate the stockade the enemy had built around the fort.

The Patriots decided the only way they could take over the fort was to run the British out by setting it on fire. The decision to do this was hard. The fort was actually the home of their good friend and dedicated Patriot Rebecca Motte. What would she think of their burning her home?

The events that took place in this historical account made Rebecca Motte a Revolutionary War heroine.

To the Young Reader

In 1780, during the Revolutionary War, Charleston fell into the hands of the British. British officers looked for a large Charleston home to use as their headquarters. They chose one of the finest, the Miles Brewton House at 27 King Street.

Rebecca Brewton Motte, sister of the home's builder, lived there at that time. Upon their occupation of the house, the British forced Rebecca to remain and serve as their hostess.

Although it is hard to believe, the following summer the British took over another of Rebecca's beautiful houses, this one on the Congaree River. There she watched the enemy turn her two-story plantation home into a fort.

Throughout these difficult times Rebecca's loyalty to her beloved American Patriots never wavered.

Acknowledgments

I wish to express my appreciation to Louise F. Aull, member of the Mount Ariel Chapter of the Daughters of the American Revolution, and to Martha Bogle and Fran Rametta of the Congaree Swamp National Monument; as well as to Marianne Cawley of the Charleston County Library, for her able assistance in research, and to Debbie Roland of the Calhoun County Museum who read the manuscript for accuracy.

Contents

1.
Loyal Patriot

When Rebecca was growing up in Charleston, she often heard her parents, Robert and Mary Griffin Brewton, and their friends speak about the unrest in the American colonies. It wasn't fair, they said, for the King of England to make the colonists pay taxes and not let them help decide how they would be governed.

It had been easy for Rebecca to take sides with the Patriots in the cause of freedom.

At the age of twenty-one Rebecca married Jacob Motte, Jr., also a Charlestonian. The couple had five children but sadly only three daughters lived to adulthood.

Trouble with England continued through the years until the war for independence began. The war had been raging for four years when the British threatened to invade Charleston.

Jacob was in poor health by this time and could not work, so Rebecca did all she could to help the cause. She arranged to have slaves brought from their Mount Joseph plantation on the Congaree River to help build defenses along the coast. She also supplied clothing, food, and other materials needed by workers and soldiers.

While working for her beloved Patriots in their fight, Rebecca never dreamed she would one day end up serving enemy officers.

2.
Occupation

The British invaded Charleston on May 12, 1780. The Patriots were forced to surrender, and the city fell into enemy hands.

British officers looked for homes to use as headquarters. Sir Henry Clinton and Lords Rawdon and Cornwallis chose Rebecca Motte's home.

Even though Rebecca was responsible for her ill husband, their daughters, and other relatives staying with them at the time, she had no choice but to turn

over her home.

To her surprise, General Clinton insisted that the family remain in the home after the occupation.

"You will," he instructed Rebecca, "have your slaves prepare our meals. And," he added, "you will be expected to eat with us and serve as hostess."

Rebecca smoothed a wisp of hair dangling beneath her white ruffled mobcap. The scarf-like handkerchief pinned at her neck was crisp and fresh. Long black gloves covered her arms where her fitted dress sleeves ended.

Rebecca held her shoulders back and her head high. She felt much taller than her five feet three inches. Just because the British had taken over her home, she would not let them frighten her. And she would see to it that none of the men were ever around her daughters, even if she had to hide them away in the attic.

Keys dangled from the silver chain at Rebecca's waist as she climbed the great mahogany staircase. She could understand why the British had chosen this elegant home with its marble and its crystal chandeliers. Built by Rebecca's brother, Miles Brewton, it was said to be one of the finest homes in Charleston. When Miles and his family were lost at sea, Rebecca and her sister Frances inherited the homes of their wealthy brother. Rebecca's family moved into this house at 27 King Street.

Mealtimes were difficult for Rebecca. Sitting at the table and listening to conversations about how the Tories would help defeat the Patriots made her angry. It was all she could do to keep from saying what she was thinking, but she managed to remain calm and poised. Her stiff, formal manner demanded respect, and the British showed her respect. They spoke of themselves as her guests.

3.
Evicted

After the British withdrew from her home and Jacob died, Rebecca left Charleston. She moved to Buckhead, her Mount Joseph plantation, also inherited from her brother.

Many of the slaves who cared for the plantation when the Motte family lived in Charleston had disappeared. Crops in the fields had died or been destroyed and farm animals stolen. As a widow, Rebecca found the situation hard to face, but she knew she would manage.

Then something unbelievable happened.

Once again British officers appeared to take over her home as their headquarters. As with the

Charleston house, she could understand why this place was chosen. The large two-story home stood on a ridge high above the Congaree River, with a view for miles in all directions—the perfect lookout for a military post.

How, Rebecca wondered, could this home invasion happen to my family a second time?

She knew she must make the best of it. At first she was allowed to continue living in the house, but a report from a Tory spy changed that.

Captain Donald McPherson, the British officer in charge, brought her the news.

"Mrs. Motte," the commanding officer said, "I understand Generals Marion and Lee are making plans to remove us from your home. We will likely come under fire. It would not be safe for you and the young ladies in your care to remain here."

Rebecca took a deep breath and stretched her body to its fullest height. She would do whatever needed to be done. The plantation's overseer lived in a weatherboard farmhouse about a half mile to the north on another hill. She and her family would take refuge there.

Gathering personal possessions, Rebecca began the move. She struggled under a load of clumsy items when a male voice said, "Here, let me help you."

Rebecca turned to see Captain McPherson picking up an arrow that had slipped from the quiver her niece carried. He was about to feel its point.

"Don't touch that!" she called out. "The arrows are poison. You might lose an arm or even your life if one should prick you."

If only he was not so mannerly, Rebecca thought, I could be angrier with him.

4.
Making a Fort

Rebecca was wondering what would happen next when the big shock came. **The British were turning her home into a fort!**

Captain McPherson directed his soldiers and Rebecca's *s*laves to cut down huge trees and build a stockade of logs around the house. Then they dug a deep, broad ditch around the stockade. Next they sawed off tree branches, sharpened the ends, and poked them out above the mounds of dirt to form an abatis. When the work was finally completed, the British named Rebecca's home Fort Motte.

Soon convoys from Charleston brought load after load of ammunition and other military supplies to store in Rebecca's home.

Not only had enemy soldiers turned her home into a fort, they had made it a military supply station!

Before long, troops under the command of British Lord Rawdon began stopping for supplies.

Rebecca learned from her slaves that some of

the supplies were headed for the British camp at Camden; others to Fort Granby and Star Fort at Ninety Six.

Rebecca went about her duties as best she could. She had allowed the Patriots to use her homes on many occasions. She counted it a privilege to help the Americans who fought for independence.

But she had never experienced anything like this. It was bad enough that her home had been made into a fort and supply station. *But to think it was being occupied by Tories who would kill her beloved Patriots was almost too much to bear.*

It was a blessing, she told herself, that dear Jacob did not live to see it.

5.
A Spy Reports

While Rebecca's home was being turned into a fort, General Francis Marion, the famous "Swamp Fox,"and Lieutenant Colonel Henry Lee, called "Light Horse Harry," were celebrating their victory over the British at Fort Watson.

Along with their report of the battle to General Nathanael Greene, commander of the southern forces, the Patriot officers sent wagonloads of

provisions taken from the captured Tory storehouse. The much-needed supplies included blankets, muskets, gunpowder, salted meats, cornmeal, potatoes, hardtack, and tea.

Now the two officers made plans under General Greene's orders to attack Fort Motte. First they needed to find out what was going on in the Motte home.

Marion's scouts knew the countryside. They also had a

reputation for finding out British locations and plans without being captured as spies. Marion sent one of his scouts to Fort Motte. By pretending he was a Tory, the Patriot soldier was able to get inside Fort Motte. Upon his return, he gave Marion a full report.

"Mrs. Motte has been evicted from her home," the scout told Marion. "She now lives in a farmhouse formerly used by the plantation's overseer. It's about a half mile from the Motte home, which you know sits up on a high plain where the British can see on all sides." The scout described the stockade, built by the Tories with the help of Mrs. Motte's slaves, and the deep ditch with its abatis.

"Do they have any cannons?" asked Marion.

"Sir," he replied, "I saw no sign of field guns, but I will tell you they have a well inside the stockade that will supply enough water for the 165 soldiers inside the fort for many weeks."

Relieved the British had no cannons, Marion shared the scout's report with Lee. They agreed a tough challenge lay ahead as the British far outnumbered their small commands. After briefing their men, the march was on.

Shortly after leaving camp, Marion and Lee had a nice surprise. They were joined by a group of soldiers sent by Greene. The soldiers had brought along a small cannon.

Marion took the lead. The Patriots

crossed the Congaree River and headed toward the junction of the Wateree and Congaree Rivers. British-held Fort Motte stood just above the junction on the south side of the Congaree.

Once there, the Patriots marched along the border of the plantation until they reached the farmhouse where Mrs. Motte was living with her niece and daughters. Leaving their men in the field to set up camp, Marion and Lee went to speak to Mrs. Motte. They found her to be as gracious as they had heard.

The generals

enjoyed tea and cakes served with more style than they would have thought possible in the crude farmhouse.

"It is crowded in this temporary home as you can see," Rebecca told the officers, "but you are most welcome to make it your headquarters. My niece, daughters, and I will move into one of the slave cabins."

The men thanked their Patriot friend for her unselfish spirit. "We will, however," Marion added, "be joining our men in the fields."

Soon the officers began working out their strategy. Marion directed Major Eaton to mount the cannon he had brought on the eastern slope of the ridge where the fort stood. Lee stationed his

men on the north hill by the farmhouse. As Lee's men advanced toward the fort, it was decided, Marion's artillery would fire at the stockade in an effort to protect them.

With the help of Mrs. Motte's slaves and others from neighboring plantations, the Patriots dug a series of trenches, where they could move through the valley toward the fort without being seen. Lee supervised the digging, which continued through the night.

The Patriot troops were all in place by early afternoon of the next day, but Marion was not yet ready to begin the fight. Before any of their plans would be carried out, he wanted to give the British a chance to surrender.

6.
Surrender or Die

Marion selected a soldier to visit Captain McPherson to ask for surrender. So that he would not be fired upon, the soldier carried a flag of truce.

"Tell McPherson," Marion instructed the flag bearer, "that surrender would save many lives on both sides."

Captain McPherson listened to the Patriot's message. Then he politely informed the soldier that no matter what happened he would hold the fort to the end.

The British officer's response left the Patriots with no choice.

General Marion approached his gunman waiting by the cannon. "Major Eaton," he said, "fire when you are ready."

The cannon belched smoke, and a cannonball screamed toward its target. Logs of the stockade shivered, but the ball bounced off and rolled down the hill.

Eaton's men reloaded, this time with a heavier charge of gunpowder. Again the gun boomed but did no damage.

Mocking yells rang out from inside the fort.

The small cannon was obviously no match for the stockade. The Patriots would have to rethink their plans.

As Marion and Lee sat brainstorming late into

the night, they were interrupted by a messenger from General Greene's unit. Taking the slip of paper from the soldier, Marion read aloud:

British Lord Rawdon is on his way from Camden with troops. Redouble your efforts to capture Fort Motte before Rawdon arrives.

Daybreak brought shouts of triumph from within the British fort. Emerging from their tents, Marion and Lee saw the reason for the cheers. Across the Congaree River campfires from Rawdon's troops twinkled in the early morning light along the distant High Hills. The small number of Patriot troops would be no match for Rawdon's fine cavalry.

Whatever moves the Patriots planned to make, they would have to be made quickly!

Marion had an idea—something he had learned in his early days of fighting Indians—but he hated to mention it. *They could burn the British out!*

Yet how could he think of such a thing after the kindness Mrs. Motte had shown? To destroy

her beautiful home! Besides, Mrs. Motte's daughter was married to his good friend Major Thomas Pinckney. The thought of burning her home caused him pain.

But what other choice did they have?

7.

A Strange Request

Lee urged Marion to make a quick decision about taking the fort. "Rawdon's troops will be upon us in a matter of days," he told his commanding officer.

"So they will," Marion replied. "But they won't be able to cross the Congaree River without first going to Nelson's Ferry. That will give us a little more time."

Marion's thoughts raced through his mind. As leader of his own militia on Snow's Island, he could have pulled his troops out and disappeared before the enemy army arrived. But things were different here. He was in the Continental Army now and took orders from the commander-in-chief of southern forces, General Greene. Greene's order was clear: "REDOUBLE YOUR EFFORTS AND TAKE THE FORT."

But how?

A single thought continued to flame in Marion's mind: *burn the fort*.

Within moments he had shared his idea with Lee. He confessed to his fellow officer the dread he felt in asking such a sacrifice of such a fine lady.

Lee knew Marion had hit upon the only quick way to solve their problem. "If it will help," he said, "I will be the one to take the request to her."

Marion gave his consent.

Standing before Mrs. Motte, Lee explained the plan. "It will save many lives if we might set fire to Captain McPherson's headquarters."

"Why, then, Colonel, do you not do so?" she asked.

"Madam," Lee continued, "your beautiful home could be completely destroyed."

"Even if it were a palace," Rebecca told him,

"it should go for the good of my country."

Showing great courage she turned to a wardrobe and brought out the bow and quiver of arrows from the East Indies. Offering them to Lee, she said, "I not only give you permission to burn my home, I give you something to make the task easier."

Speechless, Lee bowed before Mrs. Motte and withdrew to give Marion his report.

8.
Patriots Stand Ready

Hearing that Mrs. Motte had given her blessing in setting fire to her home was a relief to Marion. That she had provided the bow and arrows was especially good news.

Earlier in the day Marion had asked Private Nathan Savage, the only archer present, about the possibility of making a bow and arrow.

"How long would it take you to make a bow and some arrows?" Marion asked.

"Oh, that would take quite a while," the private had told him. "A good one has to be made from seasoned wood or it won't shoot straight."

Clutching the souvenir bow and arrows in his

hand, Marion went once again to find Savage. Drawing him aside, he told the private of the plan.

"You mean you're going to get the Redcoats out Injun-style?" Savage sounded excited as he reached for the large bow.

By early afternoon Private Savage and others from Marion's brigade huddled in the trench nearest the fort.

Marion decided to offer the British one last opportunity to surrender. This time, a surgeon from Lee's unit carried the message.

Once again, McPherson refused.

9.
The Fall of Fort Motte

Rays of the scorching, mid-day sun beamed down on the roof of the Motte home. Private Nathan Savage stood with the powerful bow. Earlier he had soaked rags in turpentine and sulfur and wrapped them around the arrow tips.

Marion gave the order. Savage reached for an arrow, touched the flammable end to the little pile of burning shavings, and the arrow point flared.

All watched in silence as Savage put arrow to bow, pulled strong and steady, took aim at the roof, and let go the string.

The blazing arrow arched upward before it fell onto the dry cypress shingles. The flame flickered and went out. Savage repeated his actions. Another flaming dart winged its way to the roof, and then another, until the flames grew bright and began to spread.

Shingles cracked; smoke billowed.

Inside the fort, McPherson realized what was happening. He also knew they would all be killed instantly if fire reached the stored gunpowder. He

ordered his men to climb onto the roof and rip off the burning shingles.

Marksmen from the Patriot lines drove them back inside. Captain McPherson knew he had been defeated. He hung the white flag of surrender from an upstairs bedroom window.

As soon as the British surrendered their weapons, Marion sent his men to the roof. Together, Patriots and Tories doused the flames. The roof was the only part of the Motte home that suffered damage.

British soldiers jumped into the surrounding ditch to reach the enemy and surrender. The few Patriot prisoners inside the fort beamed in pride at their rescue.

As always, Marion offered parole to Tories who promised not to bear arms against those who fought for freedom. Soldiers who refused were

taken prisoner.

The evening took a surprising turn. Mrs. Motte invited officers of both sides to be her guests for dinner in her Fort Motte home. It was said that she presided over a sumptuous meal with the same poise and politeness she showed in entertaining friends before the war.

Because of her graciousness and tact, she was able to encourage enemies in war to talk pleasantly together.

Captain McPherson, still suffering embarrassment over being forced to surrender, said, "Mrs. Motte warned me of the poisoned arrow." Turning to her, he added, "Madam, it would have been a blessing if you had let me touch it and die rather than bear the shame of surrender."

Mrs. Motte looked at the young officer.

"Captain," she said, "it is not a dishonor to surrender. Think of it as a sacrifice for the cause, as I did in the burning of my home."

In the days that followed, Marion's men

dismantled the log stockade, removed the abatis, and filled in the ditch and trenches around Rebecca's home.

While the men worked, a scout came to report on Lord Rawdon's moves. "When Rawdon heard his officers had surrendered Fort Motte," the scout told Marion, "he retreated, taking only enough time to blow up Nelson's Ferry. Then he hurried on to Charleston."

Under General Greene's orders, Marion moved on to Georgetown. Lee took his men to Fort Granby.

10.
A Heroine Remembered

As a result of the aid the Motte family gave friends and Patriots during the war, their estate was left heavy in debt. About two years after the Patriots defeated the British at Fort Motte, the house was completely destroyed by fire.

In spite of difficulties, Rebecca's strong will prevailed. She purchased on credit a tract of rice fields along the Santee River. She managed her property with the same dignity and cleverness she showed during the occupation of her homes by the British. As a result, she was able to pay off all debts and regain her family's fortune. She rebuilt her home on the Congaree River and continued to

divide her time between the
Mount Joseph plantation and
the Miles Brewton House.

Rebecca kept her
knitting needles in the quiver
that held the arrows of fire.
She carried it with her, from
home to home, as a reminder
of the day the British
surrender saved her house
from being burned to the ground.

~ ~ ~ ~ ~ ~

When Rebecca Motte died on January 10,
1815, she was buried in St. Philip's Church
cemetery in Charleston. She was seventy-eight.
At her service she did not receive praise for her

ability to regain the family's wealth but for her courage and character, as well as her devotion to the freedom of America.

A memorial to Rebecca is located on the site of old Fort Motte, which is private property. The huge boulder honors the courageous widow who was willing to sacrifice her home for the cause of the American Revolution.

The Miles Brewton House, also known as the Pringle House, still stands at 27 King Street in Charleston. Thousands visit the home each year and hear the story of its use as British headquarters during the occupation of the city.

A Charleston Chapter of the National Society Daughters of the American Revolution bears the name of Rebecca Brewton Motte. In 1903 the chapter unveiled a memorial to Rebecca at St. Philip's Episcopal Church.

Saluda R.

STAR FORT ●

Savannah R.

GEORGIA

South
Carolina

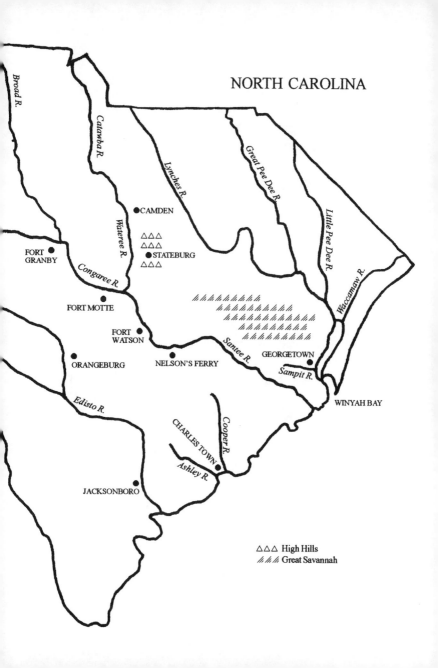

Words Needed for Understanding

abatis　　　　a barricade made from trees, placed with
　　　　　　　sharpened branches directed toward the
　　　　　　　enemy

barracks　　　buildings soldiers live in

brainstorming　the sharing of spontaneous ideas by
　　　　　　　members of a group

brigade　　　a group of military persons

cavalry　　　combat troops mounted on horses

challenge　　a task that is hard to perform

chandelier　　a lighting fixture hanging from the ceiling
　　　　　　　with several "arms" that hold lights (or
　　　　　　　candles, in Revolutionary War time)

command　　in this case, a military force

Continental　relating to a soldier of the American
　　　　　　　colonies during the Revolutionary War

convoy　　　a group traveling together

credit　　　*on credit*—agreement that payment will be

	made in the future (a method of purchasing without cash in hand)
crude	in this case, without fancy furnishings
depot	storehouse for supplies
dignity	a manner of behavior showing self respect
douse	to put out a fire by throwing water on it
elegant	characterized by richness of design and style
estate	property and possessions, often consisting of a house and land
evicted	to be removed from one's home
fidgeted	moved about restlessly
formerly	at or in an earlier time
garrison	troops stationed in a fort
gracious	showing courtesy and kindness
gunpowder	an explosive powder used in firearms and blasting

hardtack	hard bread
hostess	a woman who entertains guests
huddled	crowded closely together
infantry	soldiers trained to fight on foot
junction	a place where roads or rivers come together
maghogany	dark reddish-brown heartwood from mahogany trees
matron	an older, mature woman
militia	a volunteer group of soldiers, usually made up of ordinary citizens rather than professional soldiers
mobcap	a woman's indoor cap with a high puffy crown, often tied under the chin
musket	a long-barreled firearm
occupied	took possession of a place
offended	displeased with something another person does or says

paroled	full or partial freedom given in exchange for word of honor
Patriot	American colonist who fought for freedom from English rule; one who loves and supports his country
poised	calm; showing dignity of manner
provisions	food and other supplies gathered and stored for future needs
quench	to put out a fire; to satisfy a thirst
quiver	a case for holding arrows
Redcoats	name given to British soldiers who wore red coats in the American Revolution
refuge	a place to take shelter or protection from danger
rumor	talk not based on knowledge of fact
seasoned	allowed to age, as of wood
souvenir	something saved as a keepsake

stockade	an enclosure like a fort, usually made with stakes driven into the ground
strategy	a plan of action for a large scale military operation
sumptuous	splendid; more than enough
tact	having the ability to do or say the right thing without hurting others' feelings
temporary	not lasting
Tory	a person living in the colonies who gave allegiance to the King of England during the American Revolution
triumph	joy over victory
warehouse	a building where goods are stored
wardrobe	a tall piece of furniture that serves as a place to keep hanging clothes

Things To Do and Talk About

1. It is hard to find a great deal of information about women in the early life of this country, especially their childhoods. It is said the roles of women in the Revolution was not published until Alexander Garden wrote *Anecdotes of the Revolution*, © 1822. That was more than forty years after the war ended. Why do you think this was so?

2. Although little is known about Rebecca Motte's young life, we are told that her grandfather died when Rebecca was eight, and her family left Beaufort, South Carolina, for Charleston. If her grandfather died in 1745, what year was Rebecca born?

3. Heroes and heroines have certain character traits that cause them to act the way they do. How does Rebecca Motte show her patriotism and unselfish nature?

4. Explain the difference between a Patriot soldier in a militia and one in the Continental Army.

How did it happen that Francis Marion was in both at different times?

5. Some officers on both sides paroled captured soldiers. What does this mean?

6. Although Lee and Marion had quite different backgrounds, they understood they needed to work together to accomplish their goals. When have you experienced this situation in your own life?

7. Research sources on past happenings often disagree. This was true of how the fire arrows ended up on Mrs. Motte's roof. The way most often given was that Savage shot them with the souvenir bow and arrows. Another source said Savage hurled them. Still another said the arrows were fired from musket barrels. Finally, an officer in Marion's brigade wrote the arrows were not used at all but that Private Savage made up balls of the tar and sulfur and slung them onto the roof. What do you think? Do you think they might have used a combination?

8.   One of the Patriots fighting in the battle at Fort
     Motte was Major Maham for whom the Maham
     Tower was named. Would you like to find out
     what that was?

9.   Make a model of Rebecca Motte's home after it
     became Fort Motte.

10. The definition of Redcoats in "Words for
     Understanding" is "name given to British
     soldiers who wore red coats in the American
     Revolution." Did you know some of the Tories
     organized their own green-coated regiments to
     serve alongside the Redcoats? Some ladies who
     were on the side of the Tories wore something
     green in support.

11. Sometimes those who fought on the side of the
     King of England are referred to as British.
     Other times they are called Tories. What is the
     difference?

12. If you travel to Charleston, South Carolina, you
     may want to see the Miles Brewton House at 27
     King Street where Rebecca lived when the

British took the house over for their headquarters. The delicate ironwork on the fence is called *frieze*.

13. Gather in small groups to plan and present skits showing scenes of what happened in this story. Act them out before your class.

14. The Daughters of the American Revolution (DAR) place markers at Revolutionary War sites and grave sites over our country. What is the DAR? Why do you think they perform this service for other citizens? Do you know anyone who is a member of this organization? How does one get to be a member? Write a brief report about what you find.

15. In colonial times most South Carolinians lived in the lower portion of the state, which was divided into parishes (units of local government). Fort Motte was located in St. Matthews Parish. Locate a map of that period and find Fort Motte.

Sources Used

DAR Archives, Camden, South Carolina.

Ellet, Elizabeth F. *Women of the American Revolution.* New York: Haskell House Publishers, 1969.

Farley, M. Foster. "American Patriots.*" Sandlapper Magazine, Summer, 2000, pp 22-24.

Figures in the Revolution in South Carolina: An Anthology. Columbia, SC: Southern Studies Program, University of South Carolina, 1976.

Frazier Evelyn McD. "Rebecca Motte, Patriotic Firebug.*" *Sandlapper Magazine*, October 1970, pp58-60.

Harrison, Margaret Hayne. *A Charleston Album.* New Hampshire: Richard Smith Publishers, 1953.

Hilborn, Nat and Sam. *Battleground of Freedom: South Carolina in the Revolution.* Orangeburg, SC: Sandlapper Press, Inc., 1970.

Jones, Katherine Mayrant. *Heroines of Dixie.* New York: Bobbs-Merrill, 1955.

Means, Celina E. *Palmetto Stories.* New York: Macmillan Company, 1903.

Pancake, John S. *This Destructive War: The British Campaign in the Carolinas, 1780-1782.* Tuscaloosa, Alabama: The University of Alabama Press, 1985.

Ravenel, Mrs. St. Julien. *Charleston, the Place and the People.* New York: Macmillan Company, 1912.

Ripley, Warren. *Battleground: South Carolina in the Revolution.* Charleston, SC: *Evening Post* Publishing Company, 1983.

Will of Miles Brewton. Charleston, SC: Charleston County Library, South Carolina Room.

Wister, Mrs. O.J, and Miss Agnes Irwin, eds. *Worthy Women of Our First Century.* New York: Lippincott, 1877.

ABOUT THE AUTHOR

Idella Bodie was born in Ridge Spring, South Carolina. She received her degree in English from Columbia College and taught high school English and creative writing for thirty-one years.

Ms. Bodie's first book was published in 1971, and she has been writing books for young readers ever since. This is her seventeenth book.

Ms. Bodie lives in Aiken with her husband Jim. When she is not busy with research, writing, or public appearances, she enjoys reading and gardening.

BOOKS BY IDELLA BODIE

"Heroes and Heroines of the American Revolution" Series
Brave Black Patriots
The Fighting Gamecock
Heroines of the American Revolution
Light-Horse Harry
The Man Who Loved the Flag
The Old Wagoner
Quaker Commander
The Revolutionary Swamp Fox
The Secret Message
Spunky Revolutionary War Heroine
The Wizard Owl

OTHERS

Carolina Girl: A Writer's Beginning
Ghost in the Capitol
Ghost Tales for Retelling
A Hunt for Life's Extras: The Story of Archibald Rutledge
The Mystery of Edisto Island
The Mystery of the Pirate's Treasure
The Secret of Telfair Inn
South Carolina Women
Stranded!
Trouble at Star Fort
Whopper

═══════════════════════════════

If your school would like to visit the memorial to Rebecca Motte, located on the site of old Fort Motte, contact the Calhoun County Museum. Private group viewings are permitted by appointment only.

Debbie Roland, Director
Calhoun County Museum
303 Butler Street
St. Matthews, SC 29135
803-874-3964